The Art of Feeling

Drawing Your Way
to a Better Day!

Kimberlite Kreations

The Art of Feeling

Drawing Your Way to a Better Day!

Books in this series:

The Art of Feeling

Paper Feelings

The Write Feelings

ISBN 978-1-947751-33-0

Copyright © 2018 Kimberlite Kreations

KimberliteKreations.com

Introduction

The Concept

Emotions are tricky things... I'd venture to say that most people struggle with their emotions more than any other issue in their life.

"I just want to be happy."

"Oh, that makes me so mad!"

"If only I wasn't discouraged all the time."

"I can't help feeling this way."

As children, we learn pretty quickly how to either use our emotions as a tool to manipulate others or to suppress them so they are not an inconvenience. Oftentimes, we are as much at the mercy of these feelings as everyone else is. They come and go, defying even description. As we grow older, they begin to compound and build on each other so that we feel many different emotions at once, complicating the matter still further. Slowly, fear creeps in. We are being ruled by something unknown to us, but yet intimate to us, the worst kind of enemy.

However... There is Hope at the bottom of Pandora's Box. People are not meant to be merely victims, stumbling through life at the whim of our feelings. The reason our emotions are so difficult is because we don't know how to deal with them. We hardly even know what they are!

That is why books like this can be one of our greatest tools on this journey called life. I don't say it's a weapon to conquer our emotions, because emotions are not meant to be conquered. They're meant to be felt, and they're powerful because they are important. When a woman births a baby, the contractions are not her enemy. They are her own body trying to bring forth her child. They cannot be more powerful than her, because they are her.

The same way, emotions cannot be more powerful than us, because they are us. We don't have to conquer ourselves, we just want to put everything in its proper place so that we can enjoy life instead of dreading it.

So how do we do that?

Practical Application

First, we identify the unknown so it's not so scary anymore. What is our soul feeling? Sometimes the answer is obvious, sometimes it takes a bit of searching. Certain emotions often act as covers for other emotions, and they're surprisingly consistent. There's a book called "Core Lies" by Sarah Mae that I'd recommend for anyone wanting to delve deeper into that subject. For now though, we'll stay simple.

Our first assessment may be, "I feel mad."

But then we ask ourselves the question, "Why do I feel mad?"

Oftentimes, for me at least, the answer is, "Because I am afraid."

For instance…

I have a young child who is more adventurous than my other children. The other day he ran out in the street and almost got run over by a truck. I shouted at him as I snatched him off that street. He thought I was angry. And at first flush, I did feel angry. But why did I feel angry?

Because I was scared. I was afraid of losing him. I was afraid of the hole in my life that would create.

Why would fear lead to anger like that? Why is that actually a common issue with many people?

Let's think about it. Both fear and anger are similarly powerful emotions. They are so mighty that they affect your physical body. They jump-start your adrenaline, which speeds up your heart rate and supercharges your muscles, making you run faster and make quicker decisions. This can be good if… say… your kid is blundering into the street and about to get run over by a truck. It gives you the strength you need to reach him and save his plucky little life.

But sometimes the feelings don't go away after they've accomplished their purpose. Or sometimes they're misguided. Staying on alert for very long is a huge drain on the adrenal system, and anger often morphs into destructive tendencies if it's not channeled properly. After snatching my kid from the street, I breathed in a deep breath and let it out, then explained to him that I sounded angry because I was frightened, and I reiterated why it's very important to be aware of your surroundings. But even after our talk, I still felt jittery and frustrated. Anger and fear were still pumping through my system, even though they were not necessary anymore. Emotions have a powerful place in our life because they are important. But in order for us to have a peaceful life, we have to keep them in their proper place instead of letting them run the show. One of the main ways we keep them from taking over is by correctly putting them in their place when they get unruly.

If I would have had this book, then I would have sat down and done one of the exercises in it. I would have identified my emotions, then processed them on the paper to help redirect myself from raw emotion into a state of understanding and calmness. That would have probably been easier than going out and kicking sticks in the yard. (Though that method certainly worked.)

I'm excited to be a part of this project. Here's to improving our quality of life!

Blessings on your journey,

Jessiqua Wittman
Birth Doula and Gritty Fiction Author

How to Use This Book

This book can be utilized by a wide range of age groups. The only prerequisite is that the person can express himself, or herself, through the outlet of art, drawing - whether concrete or abstract.

There are two papers per exercise. The first paper is framed with barbed wire - this deals with the negative emotion. The second paper has a more delicate frame on it - this deals with the positive emotion.

When a strong, negative emotion is encountered, turn to a lesson. Use a black or brown art implement and draw a picture showing how you feel. When done, turn the page over and follow the directions on the other side.

Now turn to the positive exercise. Breath three to five deep breaths. Think of the positive word that is given. Draw another picture using lots of colors to show what that emotion looks like. Try to think of a time when that emotion was felt. Then turn the paper over and follow the directions.

As you draw with the darker color, project your emotions into the artwork. Allow the art to express the emotions you are going through. As you color the new drawing, allow those feelings to wash over you as well.

Feel as the art reveals your emotions - ie. allow yourself to rage with the hard, dark lines and then allow yourself to calm with the colorful, smooth lines.

Feel your muscles tense and then relax. Sometimes things can be ugly. That's okay. That happens. But don't get stuck there. Feel the yuck, but then let's move on to the beauty. There is more health and strength, love and joy, peace and contentment, waiting for you on the other side.

We send blessings and love your way. May these exercises bring you hope and help you along your journey.

100 NEGATIVE Words

Abandoned	Distressed	Ignored	Restless
Afraid	Distrustful	Indecisive	Ridiculed
Alone	Disturbed	Indifferent	Sad
Angry	Dumb	Insecure	Scared
Annoyed	Duped	Invisible	Scatter Brained
Anxious	Edgy	Irritated	Scorned
Apprehensive	Embarrassed	Isolated	Shamed
Ashamed	Emotional	Jumpy	Shocked
Baffled	Exhausted	Let down	Skeptical
Belittled	Exposed	Lonely	Sorry
Betrayed	Fearful	Lost	Stunned
Bewildered	Fooled	Mad	Stupid
Bitter	Forgotten	Manipulated	Tense
Bored	Frustrated	Misled	Terrified
Cautious	Furious	Misunderstood	Tired
Confused	Grieved	Mocked	Tricked
Controlled	Grouchy	Nauseated	Unhappy
Depressed	Grumpy	Nervous	Unimportant
Desperate	Guarded	Overwhelmed	Unliked
Despised	Guilty	Panicky	Unloved
Detested	Hated	Perplexed	Unsteady
Disappointed	Hateful	Preoccupied	Unwanted
Disheartened	Hopeless	Provoked	Upset
Disoriented	Humiliated	Rejected	Weepy
Disregarded	Hurt	Reluctant	Worried

Concerning the positive words, the ones that are in <u>italics</u> are used in this book.
The <u>underlined</u> words, are utilized in The Write Feelings.

100 Positive Words

Able	Creative	Incredible	Recharged
Accepted	Curious	Informed	Refreshed
Affectionate	Delighted	Insightful	Rejuvenated
Amazed	Determined	Inspired	Relaxed
Amazing	Driven	Intelligent	Relieved
Appreciative	Easy-going	Invincible	Safe
Assertive	Elated	Joyful	Satisfied
At ease	Empowered	Kind	Secure
Awesome	Encouraged	Knowledgeable	Self-assured
Beautiful	Energetic	Light	Smart
Brave	Enlightened	Light-hearted	Spunky
Calm	Enthusiastic	Likable	Strong
Carefree	Excited	Lovable	Super
Cheerful	Focused	Loved	Surprised
Colorful	Free	Motivated	Tender
Comforted	Fulfilled	Needed	Thankful
Comfortable	Fun	Optimistic	Thrilled
Competent	Funny	Over-joyed	Trusting
Complete	Glad	Peaceful	Understood
Composed	Gratified	Playful	Useful
Confident	Happy	Pleased	Vibrant
Constructive	Healthy	Positive	Vigorous
Content	Helpful	Protected	Wanted
Cool	Hopeful	Pumped	Warm
Cozy	In Control	Reassured	Wonderful

Use a black or brown color and draw a picture of how you feel.

I don't like to feel like this...

 Now that you have finished your drawing... wad your paper up into a ball, take three steps away from your trash can and throw your paper ball into the trash!

Think of a time when you were feeling *happy*.

Now, <u>use lots of colors</u> and make a picture of something that makes you feel *happy!*

I like to feel like this...

 Now that you have finished your drawing... tape it to your bedroom door.

Use a black or brown color and draw a picture of how you feel.

I don't like to feel like this...

 Now that you have finished your drawing...
rip your paper up in teeny tiny pieces and sprinkle them in the trash - act like you are salting the trash with special paper salt!

Think of a time when you were feeling *thankful*.

Now, <u>use lots of colors</u> and make a picture of something that makes you feel *thankful!*

I like to feel like this...

 Now that you have finished your drawing...
put it in an envelope and mail it to yourself.

Use a black or brown color and draw a picture of how you feel.

I don't like to feel like this...

 Now that you have finished your drawing... scribble all over your paper until you cannot see your original drawing anymore...then throw your drawing away.

Think of a time when you were feeling *excited*.

Now, <u>use lots of colors</u> and make a picture of something that makes you feel *excited*!

I like to feel like this...

 Now that you have finished your drawing... stick it on your bathroom mirror.

Use a black or brown color and draw a picture of how you feel.

I don't like to feel like this…

 Now that you have finished your drawing...
use a pencil and punch 10 holes in your paper before throwing it away.

Think of a time when you were feeling *amazed*.

Now, <u>use lots of colors</u> and make a picture of something

that makes you feel *amazed!*

I like to feel like this...

 Now that you have finished your drawing... give your picture to someone you love.

Use a black or brown color and draw a picture of how you feel.

I don't like to feel like this...

 Now that you have finished your drawing... fold your paper in half, now fold it in half again. Keep folding your paper in half until you can't fold it in half anymore. Now throw it away.

Think of a time when you were feeling confident.

Now, <u>use lots of colors</u> and make a picture of something that makes you feel confident!

I like to feel like this...

 Now that you have finished your drawing... put your paper under your pillow.

Use a black or brown color and draw a picture of how you feel.

I don't like to feel like this...

 Now that you have finished your drawing... tear your paper into three pieces. Wad each piece up so you now have 3 paper balls. See if you can juggle them into the trash can!

Think of a time when you were feeling *affectionate*.

Now, <u>use lots of colors</u> and make a picture of something that makes you feel *affectionate!*

I like to feel like this...

 Now that you have finished your drawing... put your paper in an envelope and mail to someone you care about.

Use a black or brown color and draw a picture of how you feel.

I don't like to feel like this...

 Now that you have finished your drawing...
put your drawing on the floor and jump up and down on it 10 times!
Now throw it away!

Think of a time when you were feeling *peaceful*.

Now, <u>use lots of colors</u> and make a picture of something that makes you feel *peaceful*!

I like to feel like this...

 Now that you have finished your drawing... use a magnet to stick it on your refrigerator.

Use a black or brown color and draw a picture of how you feel.

I don't like to feel like this...

 Now that you have finished your drawing... fold your paper into a triangle shape, like a football, and see if you can hike it to the quarterback trash can!

Think of a time when you were feeling pleased.

Now, use lots of colors and make a picture of something that makes you feel pleased!

I like to feel like this...

 Now that you have finished your drawing...
fold it up nicely and carry it in your pocket all day.

Use a black or brown color and draw a picture of how you feel.

I don't like to feel like this...

Now that you have finished your drawing...
draw circles all over your picture until you can't tell what it is!

Think of a time when you were feeling *energetic*.

Now, <u>use lots of colors</u> and make a picture of something that makes you feel *energetic!*

I like to feel like this...

 Now that you have finished your drawing... attach it to your front door.

Use a black or brown color and draw a picture of how you feel.

I don't like to feel like this...

 Now that you have finished your drawing... chew it up and spit it in the trash!

Think of a time when you were feeling *surprised*.

Now, <u>use lots of colors</u> and make a picture of something that makes you feel *surprised!*

I like to feel like this...

 Now that you have finished your drawing...
put it in your pillow case.

Use a black or brown color and draw a picture of how you feel.

I don't like to feel like this...

 Now that you have finished your drawing...
cut it into three pieces and put each piece in a different trash can!

Think of a time when you were feeling *relaxed*.

Now, <u>use lots of colors</u> and make a picture of something that makes you feel *relaxed!*

I like to feel like this...

 Now that you have finished your drawing... put it on the wall by your bed.

Use a black or brown color and draw a picture of how you feel.

I don't like to feel like this...

 Now that you have finished your drawing...
draw 12 Xs all over your paper and then throw it in the trash!

Think of a time when you were feeling *secure*.

Now, <u>use lots of colors</u> and make a picture of something that makes you feel *secure!*

I like to feel like this...

 Now that you have finished your drawing... put it on your favorite window.

Use a black or brown color and draw a picture of how you feel.

I don't like to feel like this...

 Now that you have finished your drawing... use something red to draw a large circle on your paper and then draw a line through the circle... Then throw your paper away!

Think of a time when you were feeling *playful*.

Now, <u>use lots of colors</u> and make a picture of something that makes you feel *playful!*

I like to feel like this...

 Now that you have finished your drawing...
fold your paper in half and put it in your favorite book.

Use a black or brown color and draw a picture of how you feel.

I don't like to feel like this...

 Now that you have finished your drawing... draw 8 horizontal lines across your picture... ≡   Then throw your paper away.

Think of a time when you were feeling *loved*.

Now, <u>use lots of colors</u> and make a picture of something that makes you feel *loved!*

I like to feel like this...

 Now that you have finished your drawing...
put your picture on a mirror you look at a lot.

Use a black or brown color and draw a picture of how you feel.

I don't like to feel like this...

 Now that you have finished your drawing...
fold your paper into a paper airplane and crash it into the trash can!

Think of a time when you were feeling *cheerful*.

Now, <u>use lots of colors</u> and make a picture of something that makes you feel *cheerful!*

I like to feel like this...

 Now that you have finished your drawing... put it on the front of the washing machine.

Use a black or brown color and draw a picture of how you feel.

I don't like to feel like this...

 Now that you have finished your drawing... tear it into 5 sections and roll each section into a ball. Now use a spoon to flick each ball into the trash can!

Think of a time when you were feeling relieved.

Now, use lots of colors and make a picture of something that makes you feel relieved!

I like to feel like this...

 Now that you have finished your drawing... use a string to hang it from the ceiling.

Use a black or brown color and draw a picture of how you feel.

I don't like to feel like this...

 Now that you have finished your drawing...
draw 7 vertical lines from the top of your paper to the bottom, | | | then throw it in the trash!

Think of a time when you were feeling *appreciative*.

Now, <u>use lots of colors</u> and make a picture of something that makes you feel *appreciative!*

I like to feel like this...

 Now that you have finished your drawing... spin around three times while looking at your picture.

Use a black or brown color and draw a picture of how you feel.

I don't like to feel like this...

 Now that you have finished your drawing... cut four circles out of your paper before you throw your paper away!

Think of a time when you were feeling *refreshed*.

Now, <u>use lots of colors</u> and make a picture of something that makes you feel *refreshed!*

I like to feel like this...

 Now that you have finished your drawing...
hug your paper and put it under your mattress.

Use a black or brown color and draw a picture of how you feel.

I don't like to feel like this...

 Now that you have finished your drawing... draw triangles all over your picture until you can't see your original artwork!

Think of a time when you were feeling *enthusiastic*.

Now, <u>use lots of colors</u> and make a picture of something that makes you feel *enthusiastic!*

I like to feel like this...

 Now that you have finished your drawing...
show your picture to a nice animal... a bird outside, a fish in a fish tank,
a pet dog, or a scattering squirrel.

Use a black or brown color and draw a picture of how you feel.

I don't like to feel like this...

 Now that you have finished your drawing... fold your paper into a rectangle and pretend it is a car. Drive it through 3 rooms of your house and then park it in the trash!

Think of a time when you were feeling *thrilled*.

Now, <u>use lots of colors</u> and make a picture of something that makes you feel *thrilled!*

I like to feel like this...

 Now that you have finished your drawing...
pick a person out in the phone book and mail it to them anonymously (without a return address).

Use a black or brown color and draw a picture of how you feel.

I don't like to feel like this...

 Now that you have finished your drawing...
act like it is on fire so you have to get it out of the house FAST! Run it to the trash outside!

Think of a time when you were feeling *safe*.

Now, <u>use lots of colors</u> and make a picture of something that makes you feel *safe*!

I like to feel like this...

 Now that you have finished your drawing... put it in your dresser drawer.

Use a black or brown color and draw a picture of how you feel.

I don't like to feel like this...

 Now that you have finished your drawing...
roll it into a paper log and stick it in the make belief fireplace trash can!

Think of a time when you were feeling *enlightened*.

Now, <u>use lots of colors</u> and make a picture of something that makes you feel *enlightened!*

I like to feel like this...

 Now that you have finished your drawing...
take it outside and hold it up to the sun. See how the sun shines through the paper?

Use a black or brown color and draw a picture of how you feel.

I don't like to feel like this...

 Now that you have finished your drawing... draw squiggly marks all over it and then squiggle your way to the trash can and throw it away!

Think of a time when you were feeling joyful.

Now, use lots of colors and make a picture of something that makes you feel joyful!

I like to feel like this...

 Now that you have finished your drawing...
hop down the hallway and put it on the wall.

Use a black or brown color and draw a picture of how you feel.

I don't like to feel like this…

 Now that you have finished your drawing... twist it up as tight as it will twist. Pretend that the trash can is a mean monster with a giant mouth - throw your paper spear into its mouth!

Think of a time when you were feeling *satisfied*.

Now, <u>use lots of colors</u> and make a picture of something that makes you feel *satisfied!*

I like to feel like this...

 Now that you have finished your drawing... fold it up and put it in your shoe all day.

Use a black or brown color and draw a picture of how you feel.

I don't like to feel like this...

 Now that you have finished your drawing... stomp on it 6 times and then stomp to the trash and throw it away!

Think of a time when you were feeling *encouraged*.

Now, <u>use lots of colors</u> and make a picture of something that makes you feel *encouraged!*

I like to feel like this...

 Now that you have finished your drawing... give it as a gift to your favorite toy.

Use a black or brown color and draw a picture of how you feel.

I don't like to feel like this...

 Now that you have finished your drawing...
wad it up into an oval ball so it is shaped like a potato and play Hot Potato with it all the way to the trash!

Think of a time when you were feeling

Now, use lots of colors and make a picture of something

that makes you feel

I like to feel like this...

 Now that you have finished your drawing...
hang it on a hanger in your closet with your clothes.

Use a black or brown color and draw a picture of how you feel.

I don't like to feel like this...

 Now that you have finished your drawing... make it into a soccer ball and kick it into the trash can!

Think of a time when you were feeling

Now, <u>use lots of colors</u> and make a picture of something

that makes you feel

I like to feel like this...

 Now that you have finished your drawing...
roll it up like an ancient scroll and give it to someone you love.

Use a black or brown color and draw a picture of how you feel.

I don't like to feel like this...

 Now that you have finished your drawing... slam dunk it into the trash can!

Think of a time when you were feeling

Now, <u>use lots of colors</u> and make a picture of something

that makes you feel

I like to feel like this...

 Now that you have finished your drawing... fold it into a hat and wear it.

Use a black or brown color and draw a picture of how you feel.

I don't like to feel like this...

 Now that you have finished your drawing...
rip the middle out of the paper without ripping the sides. Now throw them both away!

Think of a time when you were feeling

Now, <u>use lots of colors</u> and make a picture of something

that makes you feel

I like to feel like this…

 Now that you have finished your drawing... fold it and tape it to your favorite cup.

Use a black or brown color and draw a picture of how you feel.

I don't like to feel like this...

 Now that you have finished your drawing...
go to the sink and turn the water onto just a drip. Now drip water on the paper until the water breaks the paper. Now throw the artwork away!

Think of a time when you were feeling

Now, use lots of colors and make a picture of something

that makes you feel

I like to feel like this...

 Now that you have finished your drawing...
look at your paper and breathe in deeply 3 breaths.

If you feel this book has been helpful,
please consider writing a review
and letting others know of our materials.

Thanks!

Kimberlite Kreations

KimberliteKreations.com

www.ingramcontent.com/pod-product-compliance
Lightning Source LLC
Chambersburg PA
CBHW081336080526
44588CB00017B/2638